How Pets Changed the World

Stephanie Feldstein

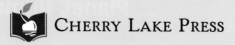

CHERRY LAKE PRESS

Published in the United States of America by Cherry Lake Publishing Group
Ann Arbor, Michigan
www.cherrylakepublishing.com

Reading Adviser: Beth Walker Gambro, MS, Ed., Reading Consultant, Yorkville, IL

Photo Credits: © Blue Creek Goldens/Shutterstock, cover; John Gerrard Keulemans, Public domain, via Wikimedia Commons, 4; © Chendongshan/Shutterstock, 6; © LightField Studios/Shutterstock, 9; © Pat-s pictures/Shutterstock, 10; © Africa Studio/Shutterstock, 11; © Prathankarnpap/Shutterstock, 12; © Durek/Shutterstock, 13; © Okrasiuk/Shutterstock, 14; © OlgaOvcharenko/Shutterstock, 15; ©Meraco63/Shutterstock, 16; © Phuttharak/Shutterstock, 17; © Maida_salman/Shutterstock, 19; © Tomas Urbelionis/Shutterstock, 20; © Ryan Brix/Shutterstock, 21; © knelson20/Shutterstock, 22; © Holli/Shutterstock, 25; © hedgehog94/Shutterstock, 26; ©bombermoon/Shutterstock, 27; © Yaya Photos/Shutterstock, 28; © Erik Lam/Shutterstock, 29; © Dora Zett/Shutterstock, 30

Cherry Lake Press is an imprint of Cherry Lake Publishing Group.

Library of Congress Cataloging-in-Publication Data

Names: Feldstein, Stephanie, author.
Title: How pets changed the world / written by Stephanie Feldstein.
Description: Ann Arbor, Michigan : Cherry Lake Publishing, [2024] | Series: Planet human | Audience: Grades 4-6 | Summary: "The pet industry has profoundly impacted our world. The Planet Human series breaks down the human impact on the environment over time and around the globe. Each title presents important high-interest natural science nonfiction content with global relevance"— Provided by publisher.
Identifiers: LCCN 2023035078 | ISBN 9781668939086 (paperback) | ISBN 9781668938041 (hardcover) | ISBN 9781668940426 (ebook) | ISBN 9781668941775 (pdf)
Subjects: LCSH: Pets—Juvenile literature. | Pets—Social aspects—Juvenile literature. | Pet industry—Juvenile literature. | Pets—History—Juvenile literature. | Domestication—Juvenile literature.
Classification: LCC SF416.2 .F45 2024 | DDC 636.088/7—dc23/eng/20230907
LC record available at https://lccn.loc.gov/2023035078

Cherry Lake Publishing Group would like to acknowledge the work of the Partnership for 21st Century Learning, a Network of Battelle for Kids. Please visit Battelle for Kids online for more information.

Printed in the United States of America

Stephanie Feldstein works at the Center for Biological Diversity. She advocates to protect wildlife and helps people understand how humans impact nature. She lives in the woods in the Pacific Northwest with her rescued dogs and cats. She loves to hike and explore wild places.

CONTENTS

Introduction

Birds Lost Forever

Stephens Island is off the coast of New Zealand. It has animals that aren't known to exist anywhere else in the world. The Stephens Island Wren was one of them. It was a small, round bird. It had a short tail and big feet. Unlike most songbirds, it didn't fly. It scurried around the rocky shores. It didn't need to worry about flying away. It wasn't hunted by any other animals on the island. That changed when David Lyall became the lighthouse keeper in 1894.

Lyall brought his pet cat, Tibbles, to the island with him. Tibbles was the first cat ever to live there. She roamed the island hunting for food. The small flightless wrens were easy to catch. She and her offspring hunted them to **extinction**.

An extinct animal is gone forever. Cats have been linked to the extinction of 40 kinds of birds. They've driven small

A Giant Industry

The world is home to more than 470 million pet dogs. And there are more than 370 million pet cats. In the United States, more than two-thirds of households have pets.

The pet **industry** is made of all the businesses that help us care for our animals. Every pet needs food. People buy treats and toys for their pets. They take them to veterinarians for health care. They spend money on training and grooming. They pay people to watch them when they're away from home.

Americans spend more money on their pets than anyone else in the world. In 2022, people in the United States spent $136.8 billion on their pets. That's more than the entire economy of many small countries. And that number keeps growing every year.

mammals and reptiles extinct. Dogs have also been linked to dozens of wildlife extinctions.

Humans have lived with pets for thousands of years. They're part of our families. They help us connect with the animal world. They help us connect with each other.

There are more than 1 billion pets on the planet. They have a huge impact. Taking care of them has an impact, too. They need food and supplies. Factories around the world produce everything from toys to beds for our pets.

Human industry has changed the face of the planet. More than 8 billion people live on Earth. People are living longer. We're healthier than ever. But everything we use or buy comes at a cost. Human industry uses natural resources that wildlife needs. It creates **pollution** and waste. It can affect human health, too. Our industries put a lot of pressure on nature. The most pressure comes from wealthy countries like the United States.

We need a healthy planet to survive. We need clean air and safe water. We need **ecosystems** with lots of different wildlife. The pet industry leaves a big mark on the world. But we can care for our pets and for the planet.

CHAPTER 1

The History of Pets

Animals such as cattle and horses were **domesticated** by people for a purpose. They were kept for food or labor. But dogs and cats chose to live with us on their own.

DNA stands for deoxyribonucleic acid. It is the code inside cells that makes living things what and who they are. It decides what characteristics you inherit from your parents. It determines what you look like. It can affect behavior. All the DNA put together makes up the **genome**. Individuals in a species mostly share the same genome. It only takes small differences in our DNA to make each of us unique.

Dogs and humans share 84 percent of their DNA. Cats and humans share 90 percent of their DNA.

Researchers examined the genomes of dogs and cats. They examined the genomes of ancient wild species. They mapped out the similarities. They learned about the ancient relatives of dogs and cats. Dogs most likely came from European and Middle Eastern wolves. Cats mostly came from North African and Southwest Asian wildcats.

Cats were domesticated about 10,000 years ago. That's around the time people started farming. People settled in villages. Villages had stored grain. They had trash heaps. Mice were attracted to these food sources. Cats hunted the mice for food.

Pets and Human Health

Sharing our lives with animals can affect our health. As many as 20 percent of people are allergic to dogs or cats. Allergies can make people itchy. They can make it hard to breathe. Pets can also carry germs that make us sick. They can have parasites that cause illness.

But dogs and cats come with big health benefits, too. They've been shown to reduce stress. They can help lower blood pressure. Pets can help people experiencing depression or anxiety.

Service dogs are trained to help people with disabilities. They guide people who are blind. They pick up things for people who use wheelchairs. They can bring people medication or a phone in an emergency. Some dogs can sense seizures before they happen. They help the person get to a safe place. They stay close so the person doesn't get injured.

There are about 45 million pet cats
in the United States.

Most cats are very independent. They like to come and go as they please.

The cats that weren't afraid of people stuck around. They had kittens that were even more comfortable with people. People liked that cats kept mice out of their food.

However, it's surprising that cats were ever domesticated at all. Most domesticated animals lived in herds or packs in the wild. It was easy for them to form a relationship with humans. But cats are more independent. They're still very similar to their wild relatives. They often can survive on their own.

Researchers believe dogs became domesticated 15,000 to 30,000 years ago. Wolves started hanging around campfires for food scraps. The friendliest wolves got closer to humans. They got more food. They had even friendlier pups.

EXOTIC PETS

Exotic pets are animals which are generally rare or unusual to have as pets. Snakes and turtles are exotic pets. So are parrots and spiders. Tropical fish are exotic, too. Some are bred in captivity. But many are taken from nature. The United States imports more than 200 million exotic pets every year.

Wild-caught animals should not be kept as pets. They aren't used to living with people like dogs and cats are. It's hard to meet their needs. Taking them from nature often hurts them. It puts their species at risk. It can spread diseases to other wildlife. It can harm entire ecosystems.

Many dogs are known for their loyalty. They stick by their owners' sides.

Doodle mixes (dogs that are part poodle
and part other breed) are very popular.

The smallest dog in the world is a 1.5 pound (.68 kilograms) chihuahua named Pearl that stands less than 4 inches (10.16 centimeters) tall.

Farming changed everything for dogs. People started **selective breeding** with dogs. They chose parents with certain behaviors or sizes. They bred them to produce offspring with those same characteristics. Today, dogs come in more shapes and sizes than any other kind of pet.

CHAPTER 2

The Environmental Cost of Pets

Dogs and cats may have started out as wild species. But living with humans changed them. They don't belong in nature anymore. They're an **invasive species**. Invasive species can disrupt an entire ecosystem.

Cats are fierce hunters. Even a well-fed house cat will hunt smaller animals. Outdoor cats kill as many as 1.3–4 billion birds in the United States every year. Some of those birds are **endangered species**. Cats kill as many as 6.3–22.3 billion small mammals such as mice each year. Dogs also chase and hunt wildlife. They harm sensitive plants and **habitats**. Pets can spread diseases to wild animals.

Some people choose to buy their pets from a responsible breeder. These people know a great deal about pet breeds. They treat their animals well and make sure their

Cats are natural predators. It is part of their nature to kill birds and small mammals.

animals are healthy. But some breeders run puppy and kitten mills. **Pet mills** breed lots of pets just to make money. The pets are kept in small, dirty cages. They don't get to go outside. They don't get veterinary care. Pet mills aren't just unhealthy for the pets. They're unhealthy for the environment, too. The poop from all of the pets can pollute nearby streams. It can spread diseases.

No matter where our pets come from, the pet care industry is massive. Companies make everything from furniture to bottled water just for pets. They make pet toys and clothes for every holiday. Everything we buy has an environmental impact. Manufacturing products takes land, water, and energy. A lot of the toys and products made for pets use plastic. Plastic production pollutes the environment. It creates toxic chemicals. It makes **climate change** worse. Climate change causes warmer temperatures and extreme storms. It harms people and animals.

Changemaker: Alexandra Horowitz

Alexandra Horowitz was studying cognitive science. Cognitive science is the study of how the mind works. She wanted to focus her studies on animal minds. She especially wanted to know what her dog, Pumpernickel, was thinking.

Horowitz started the Dog Cognition Lab. It's at Barnard College in New York City. She studies the behaviors and minds of dogs.

The Dog Cognition Lab studies how dogs experience the world. Dogs use their noses more than their eyes to get a picture of the world. It also studies how playing with our dogs affects their well-being. And it works to decode just what dogs are thinking when they look guilty.

Understanding what dogs are thinking brings us closer to them. It helps us take better care of them.

Many parks and trails require pets to be on leashes.

Keeping cats indoors and dogs on leashes can stop them from harming wildlife. We can also rethink how we spoil our pets. Choose products made from eco-friendly materials. Even better, buy less stuff for them. Most pet products are made to appeal to humans. Our pets don't care about sparkly collars. They don't know what holidays are. They want our love and attention more than anything else. Try to avoid buying them things they don't really need. Play with them or teach them a new trick instead. Your pet and the planet will be happier.

SUPER SNIFFERS

Tiny sensors inside our noses capture smells. These are called scent receptors. They help us identify smells. Humans have about 5 to 6 million scent receptors. Dogs have 200 to 300 million. Dogs can detect smells that humans can't even imagine. They can find people who are lost. They can tell if you've been petting other dogs. They also use their noses to help protect wildlife. They can sniff out wildlife smugglers. They can detect species in an area to help scientists study them.

Cats also have super noses. They have almost as many scent receptors as dogs. Researchers say they might be even better at telling the difference between smells. But cats' independent personalities make them harder to train for a job.

CHAPTER 3

Saving Lives

Pets shouldn't be bred and sold like products. Pet mills harm animals and the environment. But adopting from animal shelters saves lives and prevents pet mill pollution.

Ten years ago, more than 6 million dogs and cats wound up in U.S. shelters every year. Now that number is closer to 4.5 million. And more than 80 percent of them are saved. But that means more than 350,000 pets never find homes. They may be **euthanized** in shelters. Or if the shelter does not euthanize pets, it can't help other pets that need homes.

Communities are coming together to make sure every pet has a loving home. They're working to shut down pet mills. They're fighting for laws that create pet-friendly communities. They're working to spay and neuter pets. Spaying and neutering prevent accidental litters.

There are many animals in shelters in need of adoption.
Sometimes special adoption events are held.

Most animal shelters work hard to find homes for the animals they serve.

Shelters try to help every dog and cat find a home.
They reduce the environmental impact of unwanted pets.

Part of saving lives is keeping pets out of shelters in the
first place. People give up their pets for different reasons.
It can be hard to find housing that allows pets. Some
people don't know how to handle their pets' behavior.
Some people struggle to afford pet care.

Many communities have pet food banks. They provide food to families struggling to feed their pets. Some veterinary clinics offer low-cost services. They help people keep their pets healthy. More pet-friendly housing gives families places to live with their animals. Training programs can help address behavior problems. These programs help keep pets in their homes.

PET STORE BANS

Communities are passing laws to stop pet stores from selling animals. Dogs sold in pet stores often come from pet mills. The stores get rabbits and other small animals from similar places. Almost 300 U.S. communities have banned the sale of dogs and cats in pet stores. They cut off support for pet mills. Instead, they help shelter pets find homes.

The Future of Pets

DNA testing for dogs and cats can help predict characteristics. It can predict how the pet will grow up. It can even predict if a dog is more likely to have a big appetite. DNA can also be used to show if a pet might develop health problems. People can share the information with their veterinarians. It can help them figure out the best way to keep their pets healthy. It could reduce the amount of medications used.

Making medication for animals and people impacts the climate. It causes more climate pollution than the automotive industry. Many drugs pass through an animal into the environment. The chemicals can get in the soil. They can get into water. They can harm fish and other animals. Most environmental pollution from veterinary drugs comes from farm animals.

People care a lot about their animals. Pets become part of people's families.

People love dogs and cats. We want to see them safe and happy. Every person can take action for animals. We can help pets have a positive impact on the world. By working together, we can save pets' lives.

Activity

Organize a Pet Food Drive

Animal shelters help reduce the environmental impact of pets. They make sure there aren't accidental litters. They help people adopt instead of buying from pet stores. But they need food for the pets in their care. They need food for people who can't afford to feed their pets. Donations help keep these programs going.

Here's how to organize a pet food drive:

1. **Choose where you want to donate.** Search online with an adult for your local animal shelter.

2. **Contact the organization.** Call or email the organization. Find out what kinds of foods they need the most.

3. **Plan how you'll collect the donations.** Ask friends and families to donate to your drive. If you have a birthday coming up, you can ask for donations instead of presents. You can make it a group project.

4. **Hold your pet food drive.** Make a list of exactly what the shelter needs. Share the list with everyone you're asking to donate.

5. **Deliver your donations.** Contact the organization you're donating to once your drive is over. Set up a time to drop off your donations.

Learn More

Books

Horowitz, Alexandra. *Our Dogs, Ourselves: How We Live With Dogs* (Young Readers Edition). New York, NY: Simon & Schuster Books for Young Readers, 2020.

Keenan, Sheila. *Animals in the House: A History of Pets and People.* New York, NY: Scholastic Nonfiction, 2007.

Newman, Aline Alexander, and Dr. Gary Weitzman. *How to Speak Cat: A Guide to Decoding Cat Language.* Washington, DC: National Geographic Kids, 2015.

Spears, James. *Everything Pets: Furry Facts, Photos, and Fun– Unleashed.* Washington, DC: National Geographic Kids, 2013.

On the Web

With an adult, learn more online with these suggested searches.

"Dog facts for kids!" — National Geographic Kids

"How Kids Can Help Animal Shelters"

"Why Do People Have Pets?" Video — PBS

Glossary

DNA (DEE EN AY) or deoxyribonucleic acid (dee-AHK-see-riye-boh-noo-klee-ik AH-suhd) the code inside cells that makes living things who they are

domesticated (duh-MEH-stih-kay-tuhd) the state of becoming tame

climate change (KLIYE-muht CHAYNJ) changes in weather, temperatures, and other natural conditions over time

ecosystems (EE-koh-sih-stuhmz) places where plants, animals, and the environment rely on each other

endangered species (in-DAYN-juhrd SPEE-sheez) wild plants or animals at risk of extinction

euthanized (YOO-thuh-niezd) put to death painlessly

extinction (ik-STINK-shuhn) when all of one kind of plant or animal die

genome (JEE-nohm) all the DNA that makes up the characteristics of a living thing

habitats (HAB-uh-tats) natural homes of plants and animals

industry (IN-duh-stree) all the companies that make and sell a kind of product or service

invasive species (in-VAY-siv SPEE-sheez) plants or animals that don't belong in an ecosystem

pet mills (PET MILZ) places that breed lots of pets in cruel conditions to make money

pollution (puh-LOO-shuhn) harmful materials released into the environment

selective breeding (suh-LEK-tiv BREE-ding) choosing parents with certain characteristics to breed and produce offspring with those same characteristics

Index